# Paradoxes Of The Passion

### *and*

I0143532

## What Shall I Do, Then, With Jesus Who Is Called Christ?

# *Two Good Friday Tenebrae Services*

### Douglas E. Meyer

CSS Publishing Company, Inc., Lima, Ohio

TWO GOOD FRIDAY TENEBRAE SERVICES

ISBN 0-7880-1314-9

*These services are dedicated to my father, the Reverend Edward H. Meyer, who first introduced me to the concept of a Tenebrae Service and who was, by far, the greatest influence in my decision to pursue the pastoral ministry.*

# Preface

The following Tenebrae services for Good Friday could make use of any number of participants. Depending upon the wishes of the worship leader, different persons could be used to read the scripture lessons and do the meditations. The first time these were done, only the pastor read the scripture lessons and delivered the meditations. Enough flexibility occurs in the services proper to allow for solos and choir anthems.

Hymns were, for the most part, taken from *Lutheran Worship* (Concordia Publishing House, St. Louis, Missouri), the official hymnal of the Lutheran Church-Missouri Synod. Other hymns may be substituted, based upon the preference of the worship leader.

The events of Christ's Passion are among the most important that our world has ever known. These services were written with the hope and prayer that hearts would be touched by our Savior's sacrifice on Calvary's cross and souls would be won for his eternal kingdom. May God bless accordingly!

# Table Of Contents

# The Service of Tenebrae For Good Friday

## Paradoxes Of The Passion

The Service of Tenebrae goes back in tradition to at least the eighth century, and perhaps even earlier. The literal translation of the Latin word *tenebrae* is "shadows," and this service is presented as a ceremony that progresses from light to darkness. As each candle on the altar is extinguished, and the lights in the sanctuary are gradually dimmed, it symbolizes the gradual death of Jesus on the cross, and also reminds us of the fading loyalty of his disciples and followers. One candle remains burning, however, to symbolize that even in the midst of death and darkness, the forces of hell shall not prevail against the light of Christ! His resurrection is sure! He lives eternally! And we, too, shall live!

# The Order Of Service

**Words Of Welcome And Introduction**

**Opening Hymn**                           "The Old Rugged Cross"
1. On a hill far away stood an old rugged cross,
   The emblem of suff'ring and shame;
   And I love that old cross where the dearest and best
   For a world of lost sinners was slain.

   REFRAIN:
   So I'll cherish the old rugged cross,
   Till my trophies at last I lay down;
   I will cling to the old rugged cross,
   And exchange it someday for a crown.

2. Oh, that old rugged cross so despised by the world,
   Has a wondrous attraction for me;
   For the dear Lamb of God left his glory above,
   To bear it to dark Calvary. REFRAIN

3. To the old rugged cross I will ever be true,
   Its shame and reproach gladly bear;
   Then he'll call me someday to my home far away,
   Where his glory forever I'll share. REFRAIN

**Call To Worship** (P = Pastor; C = Congregation)
P: Lord, we cry out to You as we find ourselves surrounded by the darkness of sin.
C: **Help us to examine our lives from within, that we might see ourselves as You see us.**
P: Lord, we are mindful this evening of those who crucified Jesus, as they allowed sin to direct their lives.
C: **Help us to see ourselves in their lives tonight and to realize that we were there when they nailed him to the cross.**

**Solo**                                                 "Via Dolorosa"

**Confession Of Sins** (spoken by all)
   **Lord Jesus, my crucified Savior, I confess to you my sins, which are many and vicious. My sins nailed you to the cross. My failure to love you with all my heart, mind, and soul caused you to be forsaken by your heavenly Father. My attempt to seek popularity at all costs caused you to become unpopular. My idle gossip and unkind words caused you to be silent as a lamb before its shearers. My failure to love my neighbor as myself caused you to love me even unto death. Blessed Savior, have mercy on me and forgive me. While I know my sins caused your crucifixion, grant me a renewed assurance that your crucifixion has been the cause of my salvation.**

**Pronouncement Of Forgiveness**
P:  Take heart, child of God! Because you have sincerely confessed and repented of your part in Christ's crucifixion, the mercy and forgiveness of God rest upon you. Through the sacrifice of Jesus, you are restored to fellowship with God and given new strength to live your lives for him.

**Choral Selection**

**The Paradox Of Power**
   Meditation (followed by prayer)
   Hymn Of Response    "A Lamb Goes Uncomplaining Forth"
                                                          (v. 1)
   *(The first candle is extinguished)*

**The Paradox Of Expediency**
   Meditation (followed by prayer)
   Hymn Of Response    "When I Survey The Wondrous Cross"
                                                       (vv. 1, 2, 4)
   *(The second candle is extinguished)*

11

## The Paradox Of Truth

Meditation (followed by prayer)
Hymn Of Response        "You Are The Way; To You Alone"
*(The third candle is extinguished)*

## The Paradox Of Mockery

Meditation (followed by prayer)
Hymn Of Response                "O Dearest Jesus, What Law
Have You Broken?" (vv. 1, 2, 4)
*(The fourth candle is extinguished)*

## The Paradox Of Judgment

Meditation (followed by prayer)
Hymn Of Response        "Rock Of Ages, Cleft For Me"
(vv. 1, 3)

*(The fifth candle is extinguished)*

## The Paradox Of Salvation

Meditation (followed by prayer)
Hymn Of Response        "Christ, The Life Of All The Living"
(vv. 1, 2)

*(The sixth candle is extinguished)*

## The Paradox Of Confession

Meditation (followed by prayer)
Hymn Of Response        "Stricken, Smitten, And Afflicted"
(vv. 1, 2, 3)

## Final Scripture Reading                Isaiah 53:5

(The slamming of the Bible symbolizes fulfillment of the prophecy.)

## Solo                                "Were You There?"

## Silent Prayer

(Please leave in silence when the organ music resumes.)

# The Service of Tenebrae
## For Good Friday
### Paradoxes Of The Passion

Words Of Welcome And Introduction

**Opening Hymn**                    "The Old Rugged Cross"

**Call To Worship** (P = Pastor; C = Congregation)
P: Lord, we cry out to You as we find ourselves surrounded by the darkness of sin.
C: **Help us to examine our lives from within, that we might see ourselves as You see us.**
P: Lord, we are mindful this evening of those who crucified Jesus, as they allowed sin to direct their lives.
C: **Help us to see ourselves in their lives tonight and to realize that we were there when they nailed him to the cross.**

**Solo**                    (optional; suggestion: "Via Dolorosa")

**Confession Of Sins** (spoken by all)
**Lord Jesus, my crucified Savior, I confess to you my sins, which are many and vicious. My sins nailed you to the cross. My failure to love you with all my heart, mind, and soul caused you to be forsaken by your heavenly Father. My attempt to seek popularity at all costs caused you to become unpopular. My idle gossip and unkind words caused you to be silent as a lamb before its shearers. My failure to love my neighbor as myself caused you to love me even unto death. Blessed Savior, have mercy on me and forgive me. While I know my sins caused your crucifixion, grant me a renewed assurance that your crucifixion has been the cause of my salvation.**

**Pronouncement Of Forgiveness**
P: Take heart, child of God! Because you have sincerely confessed and repented of your part in Christ's crucifixion, the

13

mercy and forgiveness of God rest upon you. Through the sacrifice of Jesus, you are restored to fellowship with God and given new strength to live your lives for him.

**Choral Selection**                    (optional; congregational hymn would also be appropriate)

## The Paradox Of Power

The theme for our service this Good Friday evening is "Paradoxes of the Passion." *Webster's Dictionary* defines a paradox as "a statement that seems contradictory, absurd, and so forth, but may be true in fact." Not only can a statement serve as a paradox, so also can a situation. And this evening we are going to be looking at a number of paradoxical situations that took place during the Passion of Christ in the hopes of gaining deeper insight and understanding into them and also developing a greater appreciation for all that our Savior went through for us and all that he accomplished for us on that first Good Friday.

The first paradox we refer to as the Paradox of Power. The scene is the Garden of Gethsemane. What had always served as a place of refuge for our Savior would soon be transformed into a broiling mass of chaos and confusion as the Roman soldiers, led by one of Jesus' own disciples, Judas Iscariot, would invade his private prayer spot and arrest him. And as they entered the garden, John tells us in his Gospel that Jesus went out to meet them. He asked them, "Who is it you want?" "Jesus of Nazareth," they replied. To which Jesus responded, "I am he." But when he said those three simple words, "I am he," John tells us that all of these mighty soldiers, armed with their swords and spears and shields, drew back and fell to the ground. Now that's power, isn't it? Power unlike anything these men had ever seen before. But that was only the beginning.

A few moments later, when Simon Peter could not hold in his anger and rage any longer, he drew his sword and lashed out at one of the servants of the high priest. Fortunately, Peter had poor aim and merely sliced off the man's ear, which Jesus promptly healed. But then do you remember what Jesus said to Peter? He said, "Put

14

your sword back into its place; for all who draw the sword will die by the sword." Then he added this interesting comment: "Do you think I cannot call on my Father, and he will at once put at my disposal more than twelve legions of angels?"

Do you understand the power Jesus had at his disposal at this point? Twelve legions of angels! A Roman legion consisted of 6,000 soldiers. So at the snap of his fingers Jesus could have had 72,000 angels appear to protect them, a legion for himself and a legion for each of the eleven faithful disciples. Instead, he refrained from such a show of power that was readily available to him and he willingly gave himself over to the enemy. Or as Jesus put it in John 10:18: "No one takes my life from me, but I lay it down of my own accord."

**Prayer**

Thank you, Jesus, for loving me far more than I deserve and for so willingly giving yourself on my behalf. Help me now to give myself — all of myself — to you. Amen.

**Hymn**                  "A Lamb Goes Uncomplaining Forth"
(v. 1)

**The Paradox Of Expediency**

Let's go back for a moment to what some would call "the straw that broke the camel's back." By that is meant the situation that brought the Jewish religious leaders to the point where they felt the only alternative left open to them concerning Jesus was to have him put to death. Jesus had just performed perhaps his greatest miracle. He had raised to life again his dear friend Lazarus who had already been dead and buried for four days by the time Jesus appeared on the scene. Many had witnessed this miracle and had believed in Jesus because of it. So the chief priests and Pharisees called a meeting of the Sanhedrin, or Jewish Council. They talked about how popular Jesus was becoming and how they were losing control of the people. They expressed fear that Rome would soon come in and put an end to it all if it were allowed to continue.

It was then that Caiaphas, the high priest, stood up and made a profound statement of paradox. He said, "You do not realize that it is better for you that one man die for the people than that the whole nation perish." What he meant was that it would be better or more expedient to get rid of Jesus one way or another than to have the Romans come in and destroy their whole nation because of this Jesus. But John reminds us in his Gospel that this was really a prophecy spoken by Caiaphas in his official capacity as high priest and under the influence of the Holy Spirit. What he said was 100 percent true from God's point of view.

In fact, without even realizing it, he had stated the whole of God's plan of salvation, a plan that required that one man — Jesus Christ, the Son of God — die for the people instead of all the people perishing in their sins. Jesus had put it this way early on in his ministry when he had privately met with a member of the Jewish Council, Nicodemus: "For God so loved the world that he gave his only begotten Son, that whoever believes in him should not perish, but have everlasting life."

**Prayer**

Heavenly Father, thank You for Your marvelous plan of salvation, a plan that required You to sacrifice Your only Son for sinful, rebellious humankind. Help us now to offer willingly to You the sacrifice of our praise in all that we think and do and say. Amen.

**Hymn**                    "When I Survey The Wondrous Cross"
                                            (vv. 1, 2, 4)


**The Paradox Of Truth**

Following Jesus' arrest in the Garden of Gethsemane, he was eventually taken to Caiaphas, the high priest, and tried before the entire Jewish Council. After they brought in false witnesses to lie about Jesus and testify against him, Jesus was finally charged with the crime of blasphemy when he forthrightly declared that he was indeed the Son of God. Blasphemy was a crime deserving of the death penalty according to Jewish law, but the Jewish leaders had a problem here. Rome had taken away their power to carry out the

16

death penalty, so now they had to search out the Roman governor, Pontius Pilate, and convince him to execute Jesus. As Pilate questioned Jesus, he found no fault in him whatsoever. At one point in the interrogation, Jesus told Pilate that he was a king, but that his kingdom was not of this world. Then he added that he came into this world to testify to the truth and that everyone who is on the side of truth listens to him. All Pilate could do in response to each statement was shrug his shoulders and ask, "What is truth?"

And what a paradoxical question that was, for there, standing before him, looking into his very eyes, was he who once referred to himself as "the Way, the Truth, and the Life!" And even though I believe Pilate knew that deep down in his heart, he lacked the courage to acknowledge it, and so he signed the execution papers and arranged for the Prince of Truth to be crucified.

**Prayer**
Lord Jesus, we thank you that in this day and age where lying and deception are so commonplace, in you we have truth — total, complete, absolute truth. Give us ears to hear that truth, minds to love it, and hearts to follow it. In your name. Amen.

**Hymn**                    "You Are The Way; To You Alone"

**The Paradox Of Mockery**
Before Pilate issued his orders to have Jesus crucified, he tried one last-ditch effort to placate the angry mob. He had Jesus scourged. This was a brutal form of punishment which involved two Roman soldiers standing on either side of the criminal. Each one held a whip in his hand, complete with leather straps which had pieces of lead or bone fastened to the ends of them. These would literally shred the back of the person who was scourged and tear out pieces of his flesh. In fact, it wasn't unusual for an individual to die as a result of this brutality.

After Jesus was scourged, the soldiers took delight in dressing him up as a mock-king. They put a scarlet robe on his shoulders and a crown of thorns on his head, both of which carried with them

17

some powerful symbolism that we could miss if we're not paying attention.

The scarlet color of the robe reminds us of Isaiah 1:18 where God says: "Though your sins are like scarlet, they shall be as white as snow; though they are red as crimson, they shall be like wool." Scarlet is used there as a symbol for sin; so as Jesus is draped with this scarlet robe, it is symbolic of his taking upon his shoulders the sin of all humankind. As Isaiah had prophesied centuries before in the 53rd chapter of his book: "And the Lord laid on him the iniquity of us all."

The symbolism continues in the crown of thorns. The first time we encounter thorns in the Bible is in the story of man's fall into sin. As part of his judgment, God had told Adam that from now on the ground would be cursed, and instead of producing abundantly for him, it would bring forth thorns and thistles. So thorns are a symbol of God's judgment upon sin. As Jesus is crowned with thorns then, again in a mocking manner by the soldiers, it is representative of his being crowned with his Father's judgment, not for sins that he had committed, but for all the sins that we've committed.

**Prayer**

How unfair it seems to us, Jesus, that you should be punished in our place. And yet we know that without your substitution, our salvation would be a lost cause. Thank you, then, for suffering and dying in our stead and bearing the incalculable burden of our sins. Amen.

**Hymn**        "O Dearest Jesus, What Law Have You Broken?"
(vv. 1, 2, 4)

**The Paradox Of Judgment**

Following his scourging, Jesus was led out to the people one more time. Crowned with thorns, draped in scarlet, blood streaming down his face, he must have been a pitiful sight to behold. And Pilate was no doubt hoping that if this mob had an ounce of compassion in them, it would now become evident. Unfortunately, if that's what he hoped for, he overestimated them.

18

They had no compassion at all, and as their cries for crucifixion intensified, Pilate worried that a riot might break out. So he took a bowl of water and, in full view of everyone, he washed his hands and declared, "I am innocent of this man's blood." To which they replied, "Let his blood be on us and on our children!"

What the Jews were doing here was pronouncing a curse upon themselves. They were saying that they would take the responsibility for Jesus' death. And God didn't forget that. In the year 70 A.D. he carried out this curse upon the Jews as the Romans surrounded the city of Jerusalem and laid siege to it. Nothing and no one was allowed in or out. In time, historians tell us that as they ran out of food in the city, women would actually cook and eat their own children to keep them from starving to death. Finally, the Romans moved in and completely destroyed and leveled the city. The self-pronounced curse of the Jews was fulfilled.

Paradoxically, that same curse can become a prayer of blessing for us. For as we pray, "Let his blood be on us and on our children!" we are reminded of 1 John 1:7 which says, "The blood of Jesus, his Son, purifies us from all sin." And, oh, how we all need that kind of purification. And so we pray.

**Prayer**

Lord Jesus, you are the Lamb of God who takes away the sin of the world. Wash us in your holy blood this day. Cleanse and purify us from all sin and make us new again. Amen.

**Hymn**                                          "Rock Of Ages, Cleft For Me"
                                                                       (vv. 1, 3)

**The Paradox Of Salvation**

After Pilate bowed to the wishes of the mob, Jesus was led away to be crucified. Crucifixion was a very slow, painful, and humiliating death. After being stripped, the crucified victim would be affixed to a cross with three long spikes. One would be driven through each of his wrists and the other through his overlapped feet. Then his cross would be stood in an upright position and there he would hang until death by asphyxiation, or suffocation, occurred.

Crucifixions were public spectacles. Crowds would gather to watch the victims suffer and to read the reasons for crucifixion which were usually posted above their heads.

The crowd that gathered near Jesus' cross, with the exception of his mother and a few of his friends, was merciless in the taunts and jeers they hurled at him. "He saved others," they shouted, "but he can't save himself." Little did those heartless men and women know that what they were saying was precisely the truth. Yes, Jesus did save others. He saved them from leprosy, blindness, hunger, and demon possession. But most importantly, he saved them and us from sin.

And no, he couldn't save himself, for that was part of the plan, God's plan; namely, that he who was sinless should die for the sinner so that through him the possibility of forgiveness and salvation might be made available to all humankind.

And how exactly do we obtain that forgiveness and salvation? How do we appropriate it for ourselves in a personal way? Simply by faith, by accepting it and receiving it as a free gift from God — not something that we earned or merited in any way, but something that Christ alone could make possible for us.

### Prayer

With hearts overflowing with gratitude, dear Jesus, we thank you that you were willing to save others, while at the same time you refused to save yourself. Help each of us here this evening to accept salvation as the wonderful gift that it is and to find eternal comfort in doing so. Amen.

**Hymn**                    "Christ, The Life Of All The Living"
                                                            (vv. 1, 2)

### The Paradox Of Confession

As near as we can tell, Jesus was crucified at approximately 9 a.m. By noon, Matthew tells us in his Gospel that an eerie darkness came over the whole land. As Jesus yielded up his spirit at 3:00 and died, we're told a number of very unusual things happened: the curtain in the Temple separating the Holy Place from the Most

Holy Place ripped in two from top to bottom, the earth shook and the rocks split open, and the bodies of many saints who had previously died were raised to life. Certainly all of those were unusual, miraculous events, to say the least.

But one other miracle occurred that leads us to our final paradox this evening, what we will call the Paradox of Confession. As was the custom, a Roman centurion had been appointed by Pilate to handle and oversee the crucifixion. This centurion was no doubt a pagan, like his fellow Roman counterparts. If he worshiped any gods at all, they were the Roman mythological gods with names like Jupiter, Venus, and Diana. And yet this seasoned soldier had witnessed some incredible things that day. He had heard Jesus pray God's forgiveness up on the men who pounded those nails into his hands and feet. He had seen and heard Jesus deal lovingly with the penitent thief who earlier that day had shouted curses and insults at Jesus. He had seen the sun stop shining and had felt the quaking of the earth beneath his feet. And as he witnessed it all, he was moved in his spirit and led to confess, "Surely this man was the Son of God!"

Imagine that! Notice the paradox! What the learned chief priests and Pharisees could not see; what the disciples failed to recognize; what Pilate and Herod completely missed even though it was right there in front of them, this uneducated, pagan centurion loudly and boldly proclaimed. Yes, truly this man was the Son of God!

**Prayer**

Lord Jesus, forgive us for the times we have failed publicly to confess you as the Son of God and our Savior from sin. Give us the courage and conviction of the Roman centurion to proclaim you boldly before all men, realizing that as we confess you before others, you will be pleased and proud to confess us before your Father in heaven. Amen.

**Hymn**                    "Stricken, Smitten, And Afflicted"
                                              (vv. 1, 2, 3)

**Final Scripture Reading**                          Isaiah 53:5
(Following this the Pastor says, "It is finished! The scriptures have been fulfilled!" Then he slams the Bible to symbolize fulfillment of the prophecy.)

**Solo**                                          "Were You There?"
(vv. 1, 2, 3)
(May also be sung as a congregational hymn)

**Pounding Of The Nails**
(Following "Were You There?" there should be a brief moment of silence, followed by the sound of a hammer pounding. Then the organ recessional is played and the people leave in silence.)

# The Service of Tenebrae
# For Good Friday

## What Shall I Do, Then, With Jesus
## Who Is Called Christ?

The Service of Tenebrae goes back in tradition to at least the eighth century, and perhaps even earlier. The literal translation of The Latin word *tenebrae* is "shadows," and this service is presented as a ceremony that progresses from light to darkness. As each candle on the altar is extinguished, and the lights in the sanctuary are gradually dimmed, it symbolizes the gradual death of Jesus on the cross, and also reminds us of the fading loyalty of his disciples and followers. One candle remains burning, however, to symbolize that even in the midst of death and darkness, the forces of hell shall not prevail against the light of Christ! His resurrection is sure! He lives eternally! And we, too, shall live!

# The Order Of Service

**Words Of Welcome And Introduction**

**Choral Anthem or Opening Hymn**

**Call To Worship** (P = Pastor; C = Congregation)
P: Jesus, we have come to Calvary with you this evening. We seek to know the agony you suffered there.
C: **Have mercy upon us, for we caused your suffering.**
P: Teach us to endure, as you endured, the scorn of unbelievers and the torments of our enemies.
C: **Make us bold and effective witnesses for you.**
P: Save us from despair when we are circled round about.
C: **Protect us from our enemies, especially the devil, the world, and our own sinful flesh.**
P: Help keep our faith in you strong forever.
C: **When we falter, rescue us.**
P: When we forget your promises, refresh our memories.
C: **When we face death, be with us and give us courage and hope.**
P: Help us this evening to relive your death;
C: **And to understand why you went to the cross for us.**

**Confession And Forgiveness** (spoken by all)
**Lord Jesus, my crucified Savior, I confess to you my sins, which are many and vicious. My sins nailed you to the cross. My failure to love you with all my heart, mind, and soul caused you to be forsaken by your heavenly Father. My attempt to seek popularity at all costs caused you to become unpopular. My idle gossip and unkind words caused you to be silent as a lamb before its shearers. My failure to love my neighbor as myself caused you to love me even unto death. Blessed Savior, have mercy on me and forgive me. While I know my sins caused your crucifixion, grant me a renewed assurance that your crucifixion has been the cause of my salvation.**
P: Take heart, child of God! Because you have sincerely confessed and repented of your part in Christ's crucifixion, the

24

grace of God rests upon you and the blessed fruits of that crucifixion are now yours. By the blood of Christ you are forgiven of all your sins and reconciled to your Father in heaven.

**Hymn** "The Old Rugged Cross"
(vv. 1, 2, 4)

**First Meditation**
**What shall I (Peter) do, then, with Jesus who is called Christ?**
Scripture reading                    Matthew 26:69-74
Meditation (followed by prayer)
Hymn                    "Go To Dark Gethsemane"
(vv. 1, 2)

*(The first candle is extinguished)*

**Second Meditation**
**What shall I (Judas) do, then, with Jesus who is called Christ?**
Scripture reading                    Matthew 26:14-16
Meditation (followed by prayer)
Hymn                    "Alas! And Did My Savior Bleed"
(vv. 1, 2, 5)

*(The second candle is extinguished)*

**Third Meditation**
**What shall we (the Sanhedrin) do, then, with Jesus who is called Christ?**
Scripture reading                    Matthew 26:65-68
Meditation (followed by prayer)
Hymn                    "Stricken, Smitten, And Afflicted"
(vv. 1, 3)

*(The third candle is extinguished)*

**Fourth Meditation**
**What shall I (Pontius Pilate) do, then, with Jesus who is called Christ?**
Scripture reading                    Matthew 27:24
Meditation (followed by prayer)

Hymn                              "O Dearest Jesus, What Law
                                  Have You Broken?" (vv. 1, 2, 3)
*(The fourth candle is extinguished)*

**Fifth Meditation**
**What shall I (Herod) do, then, with Jesus who is called Christ?**
Scripture reading                              Luke 23:8
Meditation (followed by prayer)
Hymn                        "Just As I Am, Without One Plea"
                                              (vv. 1, 5, 6)
*(The fifth candle is extinguished)*

**Sixth Meditation**
**What shall I (the penitent thief) do, then, with Jesus who is
called Christ?**
Scripture reading                          Luke 23:39-43
Meditation (followed by prayer)
Hymn                          "Rock Of Ages, Cleft For Me"
                                              (vv. 1, 2, 3)
*(The sixth candle is extinguished)*

**Seventh Meditation**
**What shall I do, then, with Jesus who is called Christ?**
Scripture reading                          Isaiah 53:4-6
Meditation (followed by prayer)
Hymn                  "When I Survey The Wondrous Cross"
                                              (vv. 1, 3, 4)
*(The seventh candle is left burning to symbolize Christ's soon-
coming resurrection)*

**Final Scripture Reading**                Isaiah 53:7-9
(The slamming of the Bible symbolizes fulfillment of the
prophecy.)

**Solo**                                    "Were You There?"

**Silent Prayer**
(Please leave in silence when the organ music resumes.)

# The Service of Tenebrae
# For Good Friday
## What Shall I Do, Then, With Jesus
## Who Is Called Christ?

**Words Of Welcome And Introduction**

A careful reflection upon the story of Christ's Passion reveals that this is a story filled with questions. For example, in the Garden of Gethsemane, as Jesus wrestles with his heavenly Father and earnestly prays about the events that will soon transpire, he longs for the company of his three closest disciples. But after his time of prayer, he returns only to find them sound asleep. And so he asks them that piercing question, "Could you not watch with me one hour?"

Then when the Roman soldiers entered the garden to arrest Jesus, he didn't try to sneak out the back and avoid what was ahead. Rather, he actually went out to meet them, and as he did so, he asked them a question: "Who is it you want?" To which they replied, "Jesus of Nazareth." And do you remember what happened next? As soon as Jesus said, "I am he," those big, burly Roman soldiers drew back and fell to the ground, a good reminder to them as well as all of us who was really in control.

One of the most important questions of the Passion story came from Caiaphas, the high priest. As Jesus was being examined before the Jewish Council and they were having trouble finding any two witnesses who agreed with one another, Caiaphas finally took command of the whole affair and asked Jesus straight out, "Are you the Christ, the Son of God?" And as Jesus replied, "Yes, it is as you say," he in essence signed and sealed his own doom.

Well, there are many other questions we could talk about at this point, but there is one in particular that raises its head above all others, and that is the one we want to focus upon this evening. After Pilate had offered the mob the choice between Jesus and Barabbas, and they chose Barabbas, he then asked them this question: "What shall I do, then, with Jesus who is called Christ?"

Many key players in the Passion story gave their answers to that question in one way or another, and tonight we want to examine those answers and ultimately ask the same question of ourselves: What shall *I* do, then, with Jesus who is called Christ?

**Choral Anthem or Opening Hymn**

**Call To Worship** (P = Pastor; **C** = **Congregation**)
P: Jesus, we have come to Calvary with you this evening. We seek to know the agony you suffered there.
**C: Have mercy upon us, for we caused your suffering.**
P: Teach us to endure, as you endured, the scorn of unbelievers and the torments of our enemies.
**C: Make us bold and effective witnesses for you.**
P: Save us from despair when we are circled round about.
**C: Protect us from our enemies, especially the devil, the world, and our own sinful flesh.**
P: Help keep our faith in you strong forever.
**C: When we falter, rescue us.**
P: When we forget your promises, refresh our memories.
**C: When we face death, be with us and give us courage and hope.**
P: Help us this evening to relive your death;
**C: And to understand why you went to the cross for us.**

Confession And Forgiveness (spoken by all)
**Lord Jesus, my crucified Savior, I confess to you my sins, which are many and vicious. My sins nailed you to the cross. My failure to love you with all my heart, mind, and soul caused you to be forsaken by your heavenly Father. My attempt to seek popularity at all costs caused you to become unpopular. My idle gossip and unkind words caused you to be silent as a lamb before its shearers. My failure to love my neighbor as myself caused you to love me even unto death. Blessed Savior, have mercy on me and forgive me. While I know my sins caused your crucifixion, grant me a renewed assurance that your crucifixion has been the cause of my salvation.**

P: Take heart, child of God! Because you have sincerely confessed and repented of your part in Christ's crucifixion, the grace of God rests upon you and the blessed fruits of that crucifixion are now yours. By the blood of Christ you are forgiven of all your sins and reconciled to your Father in heaven.

**Hymn** "The Old Rugged Cross"
(vv. 1, 2, 4)

**Scripture Reading** Matthew 26:69-74

**First Meditation**

"What shall I do, then, with Jesus who is called Christ?" How do you suppose Peter would have answered that question? I can tell you how he would have answered it earlier that night of Jesus' betrayal and arrest. In the upper room, far away from any angry mobs and arresting soldiers, Peter boldly declared his allegiance to Christ. When Jesus informed his disciples that one of them would betray him and all would forsake him that night, good old, impetuous, spur-of-the-moment Peter stepped forward and boldly announced that all the others might do that, but he never would. Why, he would be willing to go to prison for Jesus, even to die for him if that ever became necessary. But what Peter said and what Peter did were two different things. When his allegiance to Christ was put to the test in the courtyard of the high priest's palace, Peter, the rock, crumbled, and in a shameless display of cowardliness, he not only denied his relationship with Jesus, but even resorted to cursing and swearing to get his point across.

How easy it is for us to point an accusatory finger at Peter and shake our heads in disgust at him! And yet, how often have we done the very same thing when we thoughtlessly went along with the crowd to avoid being singled out as different? Haven't we zipped our lips and said nothing of Jesus when God laid before us a splendid opportunity to share our Savior with another? And so we pray.

29

**Prayer**

Forgive us, Lord, for our faltering loyalties and faint attachments to the cause of Christ. Pardon us for our all-too-frequent denials to the rest of the world of how much Jesus means to us. Give us courage to confess his name boldly before others in order that he might confess our name before You. Amen.

**Hymn**                                             "Go To Dark Gethsemane"
(vv. 1, 2)

**Scripture Reading**                                        Matthew 26:14-16

**Second Meditation**

I suppose if there was one statement to describe Judas, it would have to be: "So close and yet so far." Think of it! Judas had been handpicked by Jesus to be one of his chosen twelve. For three years he had followed Jesus wherever he went. He had seen demons cast out of the most tormented of individuals. He had observed as Jesus made the blind to see, the lame to walk, the deaf to hear, and the dumb to speak. He had seen Jesus feed the multitudes, walk on water, calm the storm, and even raise the dead. In addition to all that, he had been privy to the most intimate conversations Jesus had with his disciples. He had sat at the feet of the Master, the source of all his wisdom and knowledge.

And yet in spite of all that and much, much more, when the time came for Judas to answer the question, "What shall I do, then, with Jesus who is called Christ?" he turned his back on his Lord, and for a measly thirty pieces of silver betrayed him into the hands of his enemies who sought to kill him.

Have you ever done that, my friends? Have you ever betrayed your Lord? Perhaps by the language you used, or the off-color jokes you told or laughed at? Or maybe by shady business deals you've made, or by failing to make your worship of him a priority in your life? We all have to plead guilty here, don't we? And that's why we all need a Savior like Jesus.

**Prayer**

With shame we confess, O Lord, that we have turned our backs on you far more times than we care to remember. Have mercy upon us. Wash us clean in your blood, Lord Jesus, and restore us to fellowship with you once again. Amen.

**Hymn**                                      "Alas! And Did My Savior Bleed"
                                                          (vv. 1, 2, 5)

**Scripture Reading**                                Matthew 26:65-68

**Third Meditation**

The Jewish Council, also known as the Sanhedrin, was a body of seventy men who came from three different classes of religious leaders: the chief priests, the scribes, and the elders. These were the religious elites of Jesus' day. These were the ones who were well-versed in the Old Testament scriptures. If anyone should have been able to recognize the Messiah when he appeared on the scene, it should have been them. But all they saw in Jesus was a threat — a threat to their authority, a threat to their popularity, a threat to the control that they had over their people's minds and lives.

Though Jesus had many confrontations with these Jewish leaders throughout his ministry, everything came to a head following Jesus' raising of Lazarus from the dead. John tells us in his Gospel: "So from that day on they plotted to take his life" (John 11:53). Never mind the great good that Jesus was accomplishing; never mind the many miracles he performed to prove his Messiahship; never mind the fact that many were being led into the kingdom of God through his powerful preaching and teaching. No, these Jewish leaders were blind to everything that Jesus was and they were hell-bent on seeing to it that he was removed from the picture, no matter what the cost.

So when they were called upon to answer the question, "What shall we do, then, with Jesus who is called Christ?" their response was straight and to the point: "He is worthy of death."

31

**Prayer**

Father, we pray that we may never be so blinded by Satan's efforts that we fail to see Jesus for who he is and what he is. Through the power of Your Holy Spirit, may we daily confess him to be the Christ, the Son of the living God, and by Your grace, may that confession be on our lips until the day we die. Amen.

**Hymn**                                "Stricken, Smitten, And Afflicted"
                                                              (vv. 1, 3)

**Scripture Reading**                                    Matthew 27:24

**Fourth Meditation**

Pontius Pilate was a bundle of contradictions. Here he was, the representative of Rome in Jerusalem at the time of Jesus' arrest. He had the full authority of the empire to back up any decision he might have to make. And yet, when he was hounded and pressured by the Jewish religious leaders to condemn Jesus to death and they, in turn, used their power and influence to persuade a bloodthirsty mob to demand the crucifixion of Christ, Pilate caved in. Even though he himself had examined Jesus and found him to be guilty of no crime, especially a crime deserving of the death penalty, he lacked the moral conviction and courage to let Jesus go free. He simply gave in to the pressure of the moment and the pressure of the crowd.

And then he did something that people have been doing almost since the beginning of time. He refused to take the blame for his part in this travesty of justice and passed the buck to the murderous mob.

Can you see yourself in Pilate, my friends? Oh, not that you would have ever condemned to death the innocent Son of God, but have you ever passed the buck of blame to someone else? Have you ever refused to take responsibility for your actions or inactions? Have you ever washed your hands of Jesus when the pressure of the moment or of the crowd got to be too much for you?

**Prayer**
Lord, we hate to say it, but we do see ourselves in Pilate this evening. We admit that we have played the blame game far too many times. From now on, help us to own up to our sins, knowing that then and only then can we become the blessed recipients of Your forgiveness. Amen.

**Hymn**          "O Dearest Jesus, What Law Have You Broken?"
(vv. 1, 2, 3)

**Scripture Reading**                              Luke 23:8

**Fifth Meditation**
What an unexpected opportunity for King Herod! Here, standing before him, was the one he had been hearing so much about — Jesus, the great miracle worker from Nazareth. He had been the talk of the land, the topic of many a conversation around Herod's palace. And no doubt Herod wondered what to make of it all.

And now he had his chance. Perhaps Jesus would put on a little show for him — walk across his swimming pool, change some water into wine, heal a crippled member of his court. Herod wanted Jesus on his terms. And, oh, how often don't we do the very same thing! "Jesus, I'll believe in you if you'll just work this little miracle for me." Or, "Jesus, if you'll take care of this problem of mine, I promise that I'll be in church every Sunday for the rest of my life."

I'm sorry, my friends, but that's not the way it works. When we come to Jesus, we come on his terms, not ours. He's the Lord; he's the Master, and even though we are not even the least bit worthy to enter his presence, he speaks to us these beautiful words in John 6:37: "Whoever comes to me, I will never drive away."

**Prayer**
Lord, forgive us for the times we've tried to bargain with You and treated You as though You could be bought or persuaded by our flimsy promises. Help us to come to You on Your terms and to daily offer ourselves as living sacrifices to You. Amen.

33

**Hymn**                           "Just As I Am, Without One Plea"
                                                    (vv. 1, 5, 6)

**Scripture Reading**                          Luke 23:39-43

**Sixth Meditation**

Sometimes it's amazing the impact Jesus can have upon a person's life. While most of the time that impact is gradual and occurs over a period of time, once in a great while it is instantaneous. Such was the case with the thief on the cross. Had he been asked our theme question for tonight, "What shall you do, then, with Jesus who is called Christ?" when he was first affixed to the cross, his answer would have surely been much different from the one he gave shortly before he died. For Matthew tells us in his Gospel that at first *both* the thieves joined in with the rest of the crowd in hurling insults at Jesus. But Luke's Gospel suggests something happened to change the heart of the one thief. Maybe it was Jesus' prayer of forgiveness for his executioners. Maybe it was the non-retaliatory way in which Jesus allowed himself to be nailed to the cross. Maybe it was the love and concern he expressed for his mother from the cross. Whatever the case, almost instantly the thief began to see Jesus through different eyes and by the grace of God beheld him as the innocent, spotless Lamb of God through whom he could gain entrance into Paradise. And sure enough, Jesus granted him that dying wish.

Is that how you see Jesus, my friends — as your innocent, sin-bearing Substitute who alone is the Way, the Truth, and the Life, the only means by which you will ever be able to enter the kingdom of heaven? Or do you still hold on to the false and futile hope that Jesus isn't enough, that somehow you have to contribute to what he has already done for you, somehow you have to earn your own ticket into Paradise?

**Prayer**

Lord, we thank You that through Jesus You have made eternal salvation a gift that just needs to be received by faith. Help us to understand that we can't earn it, we can't merit it, we can't buy it;

but that's okay because it has already been paid for in full by the precious and priceless blood of Jesus. Amen.

**Hymn** "Rock Of Ages, Cleft For Me"
(vv. 1, 2, 3)

**Scripture Reading** Isaiah 53:4-6

**Seventh Meditation**

We've covered a lot of territory this evening, haven't we? We've heard how some of the most important personalities in the Passion story would have answered the question, "What shall I do, then, with Jesus who is called Christ?" And sadly, we have seen ourselves in many of their foolhardy responses to that question.

Still, though, there's one more person in the Passion story to whom we need to address this question. That person is you. You do realize you were there, do you not? Isaiah the prophet puts you there in chapter 53 of his book when he writes: "He was pierced for *our* transgressions, he was crushed for *our* iniquities."

So what will you do, then, with Jesus who is called Christ? Before you answer that question, let me say that there is no straddling the fence with Jesus. As much as we might like to live our lives with one foot in the world and one foot in his kingdom, Jesus tells us, "He who is not with me is against me" (Matthew 12:30). So as far as Jesus is concerned, our commitment to him is an all-or-nothing thing. Either he lives as your Lord and Savior, or you cast him out of your life as a fraud who deserves to be condemned, as a charlatan who is unworthy of your allegiance and love.

**Prayer**

Lord, after all you've done for us and all you went through on the cross for us, there's no denying the fact that you are worthy of our utmost love and devotion. And yet so often we fail to give you what you deserve. Forgive us, heal us, and change us so that we might always proclaim you as Savior and Lord in all that we think and do and say. Amen.

35

**Hymn**                    "When I Survey The Wondrous Cross"
                                            (vv. 1, 3, 4)

**Final Scripture Reading**                    Isaiah 53:7-9
(The slamming of the Bible symbolizes fulfillment of the prophecy.)

**Solo**                                    "Were You There?"
                                            (vv. 1, 2, 3)
                     (May also be sung as a congregational hymn)

**Pounding Of The Nails**
(Following "Were You There?" there should be a brief moment of silence, followed by the sound of a hammer pounding. Then the organ recessional is played and the people leave in silence.)

www.ingramcontent.com/pod-product-compliance
Lightning Source LLC
Chambersburg PA
CBHW061654050426
42443CB00027B/3291